ON THE MAP

SPAIN

Titles in This Series:

France

Italy

Spain

U.S.A.

Series editor: Daphne Butler
American editor: Marian L. Edwards
Design: M&M Partnership
Photographs: ZEFA except Chris Fairclough 12b, 17t; Ecoscene 6t, 9b; Image Bank 12t, 21;
Robert Harding 26tl, 26b
Map artwork: Raymond Turvey
Cover photo: *Traditional Costumes, Andalusia*

Library of Congress Cataloging-in-Publication Data

Butler, Daphne, 1945–
   Spain / Daphne Butler.
      p.   cm. — (On the map)
   Includes Index.
   Summary: Introduces, in brief text and illustrations, the
geography, history, culture, industries, famous landmarks, and
people of Spain.
   ISBN 0–8114–3678–0
   1. Spain — Juvenile literature.   [1. Spain.]   I. Title.
II. Series.
DP17.B88 1993   92–17032
946—dc20   CIP
                                            AC

Typeset by Multifacit Graphics, Keyport, NJ
Printed and bound in the United States
1 2 3 4 5 6 7 8 9 0 VH 98 97 96 95 94 93

SPAIN

Daphne Butler

RSVP

RAINTREE
STECK-VAUGHN
P U B L I S H E R S
The Steck-Vaughn Company

Austin, Texas

FRANCE

ATLANTIC
OCEAN

• Santiago

San
Sebastian

ANDORRA

Pyrenees

Ebro River

Duero River

Barcelona

MESETA

COSTA
BRAVA

Madrid

Toledo

Tagus River

SPAIN

Valencia

Guadiana River

Alicante

COSTA
DORADA

BALEARIC
ISLANDS

Guadalquivir River

Sierra Nevada

PORTUGAL

Seville

Granada

Mt Mulhacen
11,424 ft.

COSTA DEL
SOL

MEDITERRANEAN SEA

Cadiz

N

W   E

S

Miles

0   50   100   150   200

0   100   200   300

Kilometers

MEDITERRANEAN SEA

AFRICA

Contents

The Pyrenees in northern Spain. In winter this area is covered with snow.
The village in the valley is a ski center.

The Meseta at Consuegra near Toledo. The vast, dry plain is usually windy.
Windmills were used to pump water from the ground.

Land of Mountains

The second largest country in Europe is Spain. It lies between two great bodies of water—the Atlantic Ocean and the Mediterranean Sea. It also has several islands to the east and the south.

Spain is sometimes called the country of mountains. In the west it shares a border with Portugal. In the north it borders France. The Pyrenees Mountains separate Spain and France. These high mountains run for almost three hundred miles between the two countries. Snow covers the peaks of the Pyrenees Mountains all year long. At the foot of the mountains are small towns and villages.

Most of the rest of Spain is a high, flat plateau or plain called the Meseta. In some places the Meseta has ridges of hills and mountains across it. In other places the Meseta is flat and treeless.

The Meseta is very cold in winter, especially in the hills and mountains. In summer, its flat plains are hot and dry, and the mountains are cool and rainy.

Throughout the mountains, melting snow tumbles down the high cliffs to form waterfalls. Some streams flow on to one of Spain's rivers and then out to sea.

The Coasts

Spain's location gives it very long coastlines. In the northwest, it faces the Atlantic Ocean. This, the shortest of Spain's coastlines, is rocky with sandy beaches. The weather is mild and the rainfall is plentiful. Just inside the coastline are forests of cork trees and lush green meadows. The forests make Spain a leading producer of cork.

In the south and east, Spain faces the Mediterranean Sea. This coast is warm and sunny. It has long sandy beaches that stretch for miles and miles. Because it is on the Mediterranean Sea, the weather here is warm year-round. The farther south you go, the warmer and drier the weather becomes. This coast is one of the most popular places in Europe for vacations.

As more people flocked to towns and cities along Spain's coasts, they began to spread out. In many places high-rise hotels and restaurants take up long stretches of coastline. Recently, some Spaniards have tried to put an end to so much shoreline development.

The Balearic Islands are in the Mediterranean Sea off the east coast of Spain. The weather is hot and sunny. The beaches are popular with Spaniards as well as visitors from around the world.

Cadaques in northeast Spain on the Mediterranean coast.

San Sebastian in northwest Spain
on the Atlantic coast.

Benidorm in southeast Spain on
the Mediterranean coast.

Life in the Past

Many Spanish people used to live on small farms in the country. They worked long hours to grow enough to feed their families. Most families were very large. They were made up of parents, grandparents, and children, sometimes even aunts and uncles. Life was hard, but families helped each other.

Boys and girls worked, too. Boys helped in the fields and took care of the few farm animals. Girls learned to cook and helped with the housework. They were never allowed to go out alone. An older female relative always went along with them to chaperon.

Religion was a very important part of everyday life. Even the smallest villages had large churches. A church was the center of activity in a village. Some people went to church every day. Priests were important leaders of the village. They helped people through their problems. Nuns were teachers as well as nurses. They taught the village children religion, reading, and writing.

The roads were very poor, and people did not travel far from their homes. Some never left their own village. Life in the past was very much the same from one year to the next.

People did not travel very far from their homes.

Villages grew most of their own food. They were self-sufficient.

All of the family helped with the harvest—even the youngest children.

Girls have more freedom now. They are allowed to go out together without an older female relative being with them.

People see different ways of life on television. This changes the way they choose to live their own lives.

Changes

Spain and its people have seen many changes over the past years. In the 1950s, Spain became a popular place to visit. People from all over the world started coming to Spain on holidays and vacations. As more tourists came, Spanish farmers left the countryside for the cities. They could earn more money working for the tourists. Today, Spain is one of the world's most popular countries to visit. Over 54 million people visit its cities and beaches each year.

A new government in the 1960s brought more changes to Spain. New industries started. Roads and highways were built. Many people moved to the cities and now live in apartment buildings. Spain changed from a poor farming country to a modern industrial nation. Today, more people work in factories and in the building industry, than on the farms.

As the country grew, many of the old ways have disappeared. Family life and religion are still very important, but these too have changed. Girls have more freedom. Health care and schooling are better. Families travel to other parts of the world. Many homes have television sets. People's lives are continuing to change.

Madrid is a busy modern city right at the center of Spain.

Alcázar, a fortified palace in Seville in the south of Spain, was built by the Moors.

Barcelona prepared for the 1992 Summer Olympic Games by building sports complexes and housing for the athletes.

Cities

Spain is known for its beautiful cities. Some of the cities are very old. They often have very decorative buildings that were built long ago by the Moors. The Moors were people from Africa who ruled Spain until the 15th century. Two of Spain's cities are very special. They are Madrid and Barcelona.

Madrid, the largest city, sits in the middle of the Meseta. It is the capital and home of the government. Over three million people live in Madrid, including King Juan Carlos and his family. Madrid is also the home of the Prado museum. The Prado is one of the most famous museums in the world.

Barcelona, the second largest city, is on Spain's east coast. Churches and monuments built hundreds of years ago can still be seen. There are also modern skyscrapers and a subway system. The subway is the fastest and easiest way to get around in the city.

Its location makes Barcelona a major center of trade. Ships loaded with goods leave the busy port for all parts of the world. Barcelona is also a favorite city for tourists. The 1992 Summer Olympic Games brought visitors from around the globe.

Family Life

Family life is very important to Spaniards. They like to do as many things as possible together. Most of all, they like to eat their meals together.

In summer, day-to-day life is organized around the very hot weather. In some places the temperature reaches one hundred degrees. Shops and offices open at about 9:00 A.M. and close at about 1:00 P.M. This is when the weather is really hot. People stop what they are doing and go home for lunch. In Spain, lunch is the main meal of the day. Families take their time and enjoy this meal. Afterward, they may have a nap or siesta. Work begins again when it is a little cooler, at about 4:00 P.M., and goes on until about 8:00 P.M.

In the evening, families may take a walk together through the town. They talk about the happenings of the day and discuss their plans. In cities sometimes they meet their friends and stop at a sidewalk cafe.

A late supper is eaten between 10:00 P.M. and midnight. It is usually a light meal, often eaten in a restaurant. When supper is over, families go home to bed. Even young children go to bed very late.

Spanish families often have coffee and cakes in the afternoon.
Afterward, they may take a stroll through the town. Las Ramblas in
Barcelona is a pleasant shady place for a walk.

Food and Shopping

In Spain, people shop for food every day. They like their food as fresh as possible and do not eat much of frozen or canned foods. Many people still like to buy their food in markets and small shops, even though there are now modern supermarkets. In many towns and cities, farmers sell fresh fruits and vegetables at outdoor markets.

Seafood, meat, and vegetables are the usual food. Spanish cooking varies from one part of the country to another. Some well-known dishes are omelets, paella, and a cold vegetable soup called gazpacho. Spaniards eat a lot of fruit because oranges, apples, and pears are so plentiful. Bread is eaten with every meal. Cakes, pastries, and chocolate are very popular, especially with children.

Spanish cooking offers great variety. Many dishes are prepared with seafood. The Spanish use shrimp, lobster, squid, eels, mussels, and even barnacles in their cooking.

Spain is known for its many kinds of wine. Grapes for making wine are grown all over the country. Local wine is served with most main meals. Children drink water or soda. Coffee is the most popular hot drink.

Paella is a dish made of rice, meat, seafood, and vegetables.

Spaniards shop in Alicante markets for fresh fruits and seafood.

Going to School

Spain's public schools are run by the government. Schooling is free to everyone. There are many private schools, too. Some are religious and some are not. At religious schools parents may pay a small fee. Boys and girls usually go to separate schools. They often wear uniforms.

All children must go to school when they are six years old. They must stay at least until they are fourteen years old. Today, almost all four- and five-year-olds are in preschool. Preschool is voluntary. That is, children do not have to attend.

Schools are open from Monday to Friday. The school day starts at 9:00 A.M. and stops at 1:00 P.M. for lunch. It then starts again at 3:00 P.M. and finishes at 5:00 P.M. Children who are unable to go home for lunch have a typical family meal at school. At many schools transportation to school and lunches are usually free.

The school day is very long for these children, but they have long vacations, too. They have as much as three months off in the summer. Several two-week vacations during the school year give children more time off.

Primary school children and their teacher in the classroom.

A festival in Alicante celebrating the struggle between Christians and Moors.
Children dress up in traditional Spanish costumes, and spectators line the streets.

Leisure Time

Festivals, called fiestas, play a big role in Spanish life. There is a fiesta for every occasion. People dress up in colorful costumes. Streets and buildings are decorated. There are parades and firework displays. Some fiestas celebrate religious holidays. Everyone celebrates Easter week. In addition, each town and city has its own fiestas to honor events and saints.

Spaniards spend some of their leisure time enjoying sports. Soccer is the most popular sport. Most cities have a soccer stadium. The stadium in Madrid is one of the largest in the world. Bullfighting is also popular, although some people believe it is cruel and want to see it stopped.

There is a wide range of other sports, too. Spaniards like tennis, golf, and a ball game called pelota or jai alai. Bicycling is another well-liked sport. Thousands of cyclers turn out each year for Madrid's bicycle day.

Most people take their vacations in August. Small shops and stores close down for the whole month. Families head for the beaches along the Mediterranean coast and on the Balearic Islands. There they enjoy sailing, boating, and swimming. In winter, there is skiing in the mountains.

Farming and Fishing

More than half of the land in Spain is used as farmland. Part of the farmland is used for raising crops. The rest is used as pasture land for cattle, goats, and other livestock.

In some places poor soil and little rainfall made it hard to grow some crops. Then a system was developed to bring water to the land. Now huge amounts of fruits and vegetables are grown. A great deal is sold to other countries. There are orchards of apples, peaches, and pears in the north. Oranges, lemons, and grapefruit grow well in the south. Fields of wheat and barley are seen throughout the country. Spain is also a leading grower of olives and grapes.

Thousands of people work in the fishing industry. They work on the fishing boats and in the fish processing factories. Spain's fishing fleet is the third largest in Europe. It fishes off both the Atlantic and Mediterranean coasts.

Tons of mussels, crabs, shrimps, and lobsters are caught each year. Also cod, tuna, and sardines. Some of this seafood is served in Spain's homes and restaurants. The rest is shipped around the world.

Oranges ripen well in the warm
Spanish sunshine.

Modern grape-picking machinery
helps farmers with the harvest.

By using modern methods, Spanish farmers can make their crops
grow well even on very dry land.

Ship building in Cadiz.

Chemical factory in Barcelona.

Leather goods and ceramic pots and tiles are made in traditional designs and exported.

New Industries

Tourism has completely changed Spain. More people visit Spain each year than actually live there. Tourists spend money for meals, places to stay, and sightseeing. Taking care of these visitors creates many good jobs for hardworking Spaniards.

Although tourism is still the most important industry, new industries have started up. Spain builds ships, cars, and bicycles. Busy factories produce large amounts of cement and chemicals. Ceramic goods such as decorative plates and tiles are a big industry. Ceramics are made out of minerals such as clay. They are baked at very high temperatures.

Cotton and wool, and leather shoes and handbags are all important to Spanish industry. In addition, Spain is one of the world's biggest producers of cork.

All of these industries have made life better for the people of Spain. But there are some problems, too. In some places the country is suffering from pollution. It makes the air, water, and soil dirty. People have begun to discuss how to clean up the pollution. They are learning ways to put an end to the problem.

Famous Landmarks

Columbus set sail from Spain to discover America in 1492. Today his statue points out to sea.

The Palacio Real (Royal Palace) in Madrid was built by Philip V in the 18th century. It has 2,800 rooms and is now a museum.

The Cathedral of Santiago de
Compostela in Santiago.

The Casa Battlló in Barcelona—work of the
20th century architect, Antonio Gaudí.

Gardens in the Alhambra Palace,
Granada. This was the last stronghold
of the Moors in the 15th century.

El Escorial near Madrid was built by
Philip II in the 16th century. Part palace
and part monastery, it is now a museum.

Facts and Figures

Spain—the Land and People

Population:	39,479,000
Area:	195,000 square miles
Capital City:	Madrid
Population:	4,000,000
Language:	Spanish, also Catalan and Basque
Religion:	Roman Catholic

Main Public Holidays

New Year's Day	January 1
Epiphany	January 6
Holy Thursday	date varies
Good Friday	date varies
Labor Day	May 1
Corpus Christi	June 6
Feast of Santiago	July 25
The Assumption	August 15
All Saints' Day	November 1
Constitution Day	December 6
Christmas Day	December 25

Hours and Money

School Hours:	9:00 A.M. to 1:00 P.M. 4:30 P.M. to 6:00 P.M. Monday to Friday
Shopping and Business Hours:	9:00 A.M. to 1:00 P.M. 4:00 to 8:00 P.M.
Money:	Pesetas (100 pesetas are about $1.00)

Landmarks

Highest mountain:	Mulhacen in the Sierra Nevada 11,424 ft.
Longest rivers:	Ebro Guadalquivir

Some Useful Spanish Words

hello	hola	yes	sí
goodbye	adiós	no	no
please	por favor	mister	señor
thank you	gracias	madam	señora

Average Temperatures in Fahrenheit

	January	June
Barcelona (northeast)	46°F	73°F
Madrid (center)	40°F	77°F
Santiago (northwest)	45°F	64°F

Further Reading

Getting to Know Spain, National Textbook, 1989
James, Ian. *Spain*. Watts, 1989
Lye, Keith. *Passport to Spain*. Watts, 1987
Miller, Arthur. *Spain*. Chelsea House, 1989

Audio-Visual and Language

Daizovi, Lonnie G. and Saxon, Ed. *Spanish Alive*, Level 1. Songbook and cassette, 1990.
Hazzan, Anne-Francoise. *Let's Learn Spanish Coloring Book*. National Textbook, 1988.
Mahoney, Judy and Cronan, Mary. *Teach Me More Spanish*. Teach Me Tapes, Inc., 1989.

Index